Skin Care

Perspectives on Physical Health

by Susan R. Gregson

Consultant:
Charles E. Crutchfield III, MD
Clinical Assistant Professor of Dermatology
University of Minnesota

LifeMatters
an imprint of Capstone Press
Mankato, Minnesota

LifeMatters Books are published by Capstone Press
PO Box 669 • 151 Good Counsel Drive • Mankato, Minnesota 56002
http://www.capstone-press.com

Printed in the United States of America

Library of Congress Cataloging-in-Publication Data
Gregson, Susan R.
    Skin care / by Susan R. Gregson.
          p.   cm.—(Perspectives on physical health)
    Includes bibliographical references and index.
    Summary: Discusses different aspects of skin care, emphasizing the two skin conditions that affect teenagers the most: acne and sun damage.
    ISBN 0-7368-0419-6 (book)—ISBN 0-7368-0438-2 (series)
    1. Skin—Care and hygiene—Juvenile literature. 2. Teenagers—Health and hygiene—Juvenile literature. [1. Skin—Care and hygiene. 2. Acne.] I. Title. II. Series.
    RL87 .G69 2000
    616.5—dc21   99-055031
                                    CIP

Staff Credits
Rebecca Aldridge, editor; Adam Lazar, designer; Jodi Theisen, photo researcher

Photo Credits
Cover: PNI/©RubberBall
FPG International/©VCG, 58
Index Stock Photography/8, 38, 40
International Stock/©Scott Barrow, 26; ©James Davis, 33
Photri, Inc./©Fotopic, 11, 53; ©Raymond, 17; ©Sisse Jarner, 25; ©Irene Vandermolen, 35; ©Vic Bider, 46
Unicorn Stock Photos/©Charles E. Schmidt, 7; ©Jeff Greenberg, 21
Uniphoto/28; ©Jackson Smith, 18; ©Bob Daemmrich, 43; ©Mitch Diamond, 50, 57
Visuals Unlimited/©Ken Greer, 14; ©Kjell B. Sandved, 49

ADP-0367

Table of Contents

Chapter
Overview

Skin is the body's largest organ. It protects the body and controls body temperature among other things.

The three main layers of skin are the epidermis, the dermis, and the subcutaneous layers.

Acne is the most common skin problem.

Sun damage to a teen's skin now can affect him or her later in life.

Chapter 1

The Skin Story

The Body's Protector

Skin is the body's largest organ. It covers a person from head to toe. Skin is waterproof. That's why water beads up on the skin when a person showers or swims. Skin protects other organs, muscles, and tissues from dirt and germs.

The skin has more than 4 million pores.

Temperature Control

Skin not only protects what is inside the body but also helps control body temperature. When a person gets hot, sweat glands in the skin make perspiration, or sweat. Perspiration rises to the skin's surface through the pores. These are tiny holes that are visible on the skin. Once perspiration hits the top layer of skin it evaporates into the air. This process of a liquid changing to a vapor cools the body. While a person works up a sweat, the body also tries to cool off by telling blood vessels to grow larger. The body loses heat faster when blood flows closer to the surface of the skin.

When a person feels cold, the blood vessels in the skin shrink. Blood does not flow as easily. Because the blood is further away from the skin's surface, the body does not lose as much heat. Sometimes when the blood vessels shrink, tiny muscles nearby shrink around the hair root in the skin. This causes lots of little bumps on the skin called goose bumps or goose pimples.

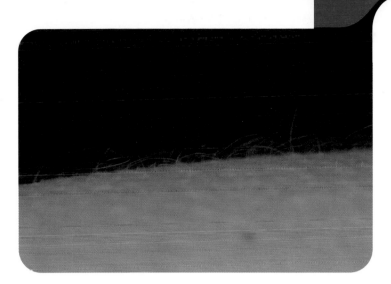

Skin Sense

Skin helps people sense changes going on around the body. It senses heat and cold. For example, skin tells people when they are standing too close to a roaring fire. It tells people when they are touching an ice cube. Skin also senses pressure and pain. It tells the brain when a person has bumped into something. It also signals the brain when a person is hurt. Skin sends a message to the brain. In turn, the brain tells the body what to do. The brain might say, "Hey, it's cold out. Put on a coat." Not all the messages from skin are bad ones. Skin helps people feel soft, warm towels; cool, soothing lotions; and tickling fingers, too.

D—lightful Skin

Chemicals in the skin work with sunlight to make vitamin D. This vitamin helps growth and development. The body needs vitamin D to help it absorb calcium for strong bones.

A Window to the Body

Skin acts like a window into the body. Skin can give a doctor clues about what is going on in a person's body. An itchy, red rash could mean the person has chicken pox. Such a rash also could be a reaction to a certain food or medicine. Yellowish skin could mean the person has a liver disease. Skin that looks a grayish, greenish-yellow color is called sallow skin. This could be a sign of drug use.

The Skin You're In

Take a look at your arm. The skin you see is only part of the skin you're in. The skin has three layers. The layer you can look at is called the epidermis. Most of the epidermis is made of live skin cells. However, the very upper part of the epidermis consists of dead skin cells.

The body makes new skin cells all the time. It takes 28 days for skin cells to form and push up to the top layer of skin. If you rub your skin hard enough, the dead, flaky cells of the upper epidermis come off. If you skin your knee, the epidermis often is rubbed off. Then you can see pinker, living skin cells underneath. These living cells are the top of the skin layer known as the dermis.

An area of skin just a little larger than a quarter contains 600 sweat glands, 100 oil glands, 100 fat glands, 65 hairs, and 20 blood vessels.

The dermis is the middle layer of skin. Sweat glands, oil glands, nerves, and blood vessels run through the dermis. Sweat glands make sweat to help cool the body. Oil, or sebaceous, glands help keep skin smooth and elastic. Nerves send messages to the brain about what the skin is feeling. Blood vessels help control body temperature.

The subcutaneous layer is the deepest layer of the skin. It connects the skin to the muscles. This deep layer of skin is made of fatty tissue that cushions the body. The fatty tissue also helps keep body temperature even.

Teen Skin

Skin is an important organ that people sometimes take for granted. How the skin looks and feels affects people physically and psychologically, or mentally. How skin looks has a lot to do with self-esteem and how people feel about their appearance. Teens, especially, worry about their looks. If teens think they don't look good, they often don't feel good about themselves.

Skin makes up about 15 percent of a person's body weight. Skin is thinnest on the eyelid and thickest on the bottom of the feet.

Betsy's face is covered with freckles. She also has a few red pimples. Betsy hates the way she looks. In the morning, Betsy stands in front of her bedroom window. She combs her hair using her shadow on the wall. She doesn't like to look at herself in the mirror.

BETSY, AGE 15

Two skin conditions affect teens the most. Acne is the most visible and common skin condition treated by doctors. Some teens have mild acne or a few bothersome pimples now and then. Other teens may have large, red pimples all over their face, back, shoulders, and chest. Both mild and severe acne can make a person feel embarrassed or ashamed. Some acne can be physically painful, too. Luckily, both forms of acne can be treated successfully.

The other skin condition that will most affect teens is sun damage. The effects of too much sun may not show up in the teen years, but they usually appear later in life. Damage to the skin occurs in the teen years. Protecting the skin as a teen can help a person to look healthy later in life. An awesome tan now likely will mean dried and wrinkled skin by middle age. Even worse, sun damage now can lead to skin cancer later.

Points to Consider

Which layer of the skin sends messages to the brain about the things you feel such as pain, pleasure, heat, and cold?

What are at least two reasons why skin is important to the body?

How do you feel about your skin?

Acne is blocked pores. The different types of acne are whiteheads, blackheads, pimples, cysts, and nodules.

Almost every teen gets acne because it is related to the hormones in maturing bodies. Some adults get acne, too.

If skin pores clog, a person gets whiteheads or blackheads. If a follicle wall breaks, the body fights bacteria, which causes red, pus-filled pimples.

Acne is hormone-related. However, many things can make acne worse, including stress, makeup, and rarely, food reactions.

Chapter **2**

Acne

Doctors use the term *acne vulgaris,* which means common acne.
Many people call acne pimples or zits. There are different types
of acne. Some acne consists of blocked pores called whiteheads
or blackheads. Some acne appears as red, bumpy pimples that
sometimes have yellow tops. Deep, lumpy, painful knots in the
skin are the worst kind of acne. These lumps are called nodules
or cysts.

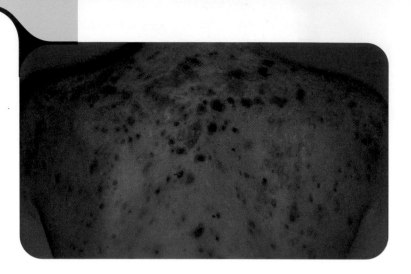

Acne most often occurs on the face. However, people can get acne on the neck, chest, shoulders, and back. These areas of the body have the most sebaceous glands. These glands are involved in causing acne. Acne can even show up wherever people sweat a lot, such as the armpits. Some people get acne outbreaks after exercise.

Who Gets Acne?

Acne affects most teens and some adults. In the majority of cases, acne clears up, even if just left alone. However, this can take years. In the meantime, a person may feel horrible about himself or herself. In some cases, a person may get permanent scars.

Both boys and girls get acne, but the acne may be worse for them at different ages. Acne is hormone-related. Hormones are body chemicals that affect sexual growth and development and control body functions. Changing hormones are a part of a teen's life as the body matures. Hormone levels in adults can change, too. The change might be related to menstruation. This is the monthly discharge of blood, fluids, and tissue from the uterus in nonpregnant females. The uterus is where an unborn baby grows and develops. Hormone changes also may be related to stress.

Almost every teen in the world gets acne. Some studies estimate that 90 percent of teens get the skin condition at some time. The National Center for Health Statistics reports that only 28 percent of kids ages 12 to 17 have clear skin.

Acne can be hereditary, or passed from parents to their children. However, experts do not know how much heredity affects acne because almost all teens get acne. If both of a teen's parents had acne, most likely that teen will have acne, too.

Another factor in acne is the strength of a person's follicle walls. A follicle is a little sac and canal under the skin that fills with oil, bacteria, and dead skin cells. The follicle starts under the skin and goes all the way to the surface. Often the follicle contains a hair that pokes through a pore in the skin.

If follicle walls are weak, they burst easily and bacteria leak into the surrounding skin. The body attacks the bacteria. This creates a red, swollen bump—a pimple. People with strong follicle walls tend to get more blackheads and whiteheads than they do pimples. The oil, bacteria, and skin cells move from the follicle to the skin's surface. The follicle wall, however, does not break.

The word *acne* comes from a Greek word that means eruption of the face.

Vance looked in the mirror after his morning shower. One, two, three, four, five, six. He counted six pimples on his forehead. One was right between his eyebrows. "No way am I doing school pictures today," Vance said to himself. He groaned and tried to comb his hair over the worst zits.

VANCE, AGE 16

Whiteheads and Blackheads

Many people believe that unclean skin causes acne. This belief is false. Acne starts in the sebaceous glands. During the teen years, sex hormone levels in the body increase. Hormones kick the sebaceous glands into gear. Sometimes the hormones kick just a little too hard. Most sebaceous glands are located on the face, upper back, and chest. These areas are the same places people tend to get acne.

As hormone levels increase, oil glands get bigger. They also make an oily material called sebum. Skin needs sebum to make it healthy and flexible, but a teen's body often makes too much sebum. Sebum moves from the oil glands through the skin's follicles and to the skin's surface. The skin becomes oily and shiny. Even hair can get oily and limp as sebum moves into the scalp.

Sebum acts below the skin's surface. Here it makes the cells in the follicles shed more quickly. The dead cells clump together. The sebum, the dead skin cells, and some bacteria block the follicle and pore.

When pores become blocked, the skin bulges and a whitehead appears. If the top of the stuff blocking the pore breaks through the skin, the result is a blackhead. Blackheads are not dirt. They are dead skin cells and oil exposed to air. When these substances oxidize, they change color. This is the same process that occurs when iron is exposed to air, changes color, and rusts. The skin and oil pick up melanin near the skin's surface. Melanin is a chemical that determines the skin's lightness or darkness. Melanin also contributes to the darkness of blackheads.

Pimples

Bacteria also can cause pimples. The dead skin cells and oil make a good environment for growing bacteria. It's normal to have bacteria on the skin cells. The bacteria, sebum, and skin cells may cause the follicle wall to break. If this happens, bacteria get into the skin near the follicle. The body then attacks the bacteria.

Usually, a red and swollen bump appears near the spot where the bacteria entered the skin. Often the bump has a yellow top. The yellow top is the white blood cells attacking the bacteria. Think about the last time you got a cut and it became infected. For a while, the cut probably was red, swollen, and itchy. The redness indicated your body was sending extra white blood cells to fight bacteria.

Sometimes, oil glands keep pumping, but the follicle wall does not break. The sebum and skin cells do not move to the surface to become a blackhead or whitehead. Instead, the sebum and skin cells collect under the skin. This creates a soft lump under the skin called a cyst. A cyst usually is not painful unless it becomes infected. Some people get large, deep pockets of swelling and infection called nodules. Acne this severe can leave scars, pockmarks, and craters in the skin.

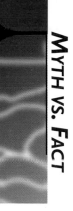
Myth: Almost everyone gets pimples, so it's no big deal.

Fact: Experts surveyed teens with pimples. Almost half of these teens said that their acne affects the way people react toward them.

Acne Agitators

Some things can agitate acne and make it worse. One of the biggest myths about acne is that eating certain foods causes it. Studies, however, have shown that sometimes eating particular foods can make acne worse. For example, some people may notice that eating chocolate, greasy foods, or another particular food seems to worsen acne. In cases like these, people should try to avoid eating their acne trigger food or foods.

Another acne myth is that scrubbing the skin several times a day keeps it clean and acne-free. In fact, the opposite is true. Washing the skin too often or too hard can cause the oil glands to produce too much sebum. It is a good idea to wash the face daily. This helps to remove dirt that can block pores. However, a gentle wash two times a day should be enough. Scrubbing the face hard may make a person feel he or she is getting the skin really clean. Scrubbing, however, irritates the skin and can make acne worse.

Other acne agitators include:

Sweating. Sweating helps oil and skin cells in follicles to clump together. Sweat can aid bacteria growth, too.

Oil-based makeup. Teen bodies produce more than enough oil. Putting even more oil on the skin can make acne worse.

Stress and strong emotions. Stress makes hormone levels bounce up and down. Changes in hormone levels can mean acne. Strong emotions such as anxiety and worry increase feelings of stress. A person may seem to get more zits right before a big test or a hot date. This may not be his or her imagination.

Menstrual cycle. Girls sometimes get more acne around and during the time of their periods. Once again, shifting hormone levels are at work.

Dirt, oil, and grease. These substances all can block pores and add to acne agony. For example, sweating over a fast-food french fry machine can make acne worse.

Skin Care

Points to Consider

How many times a day do you wash your face? Do you think this makes your skin better or worse? Why?

What is the difference between whiteheads, blackheads, and pimples?

Think about the last time you had a bad breakout. What do you think were your acne agitators?

You can take steps to control acne.

Not squeezing blemishes, keeping skin clean, and avoiding grease and other acne agitators all can lessen acne.

The sun does not help acne.

Working to control acne can help a person look and feel better.

Chapter **3**

Self-Help for Acne

Right now you may be thinking, "It's hopeless. I get zits. Everyone gets zits. I'll just hide my head under a paper bag until I'm 25." It's natural to think this way, but you don't have to do it for long. You can take action to get acne under control. Some acne may not improve after trying the following self-help steps. If this is the case, then trying acne medications may improve acne. The bottom line is, you don't have to wait for acne to go away.

"The easiest way to wash your face is with your hands. Lather your hands with a mild soap. Gently rub your hands in circles around your face, chin, and neck. Rinse carefully with warm water. Be sure to wash off all of the soap, especially at your neck. Pat your face dry with a towel. If you like to use a washcloth on your face, be sure to use a clean one every day. Bacteria can really grow on a damp washcloth. Yuck!"
—Barbara, age 14

MALIK, AGE 13

Malik noticed some small bumps on his skin. His older sister, Ashley, told him the bumps were pimples. The next time Malik went to his doctor, he pointed out the pimples on his forehead and face. The doctor told him that he had mild acne. Malik said the zits made him feel like he had a dirty face. He told the doctor that he sometimes squeezed his pimples because he wanted them to go away faster.

Skin Care

Many people have popped or squeezed a zit at one time or another. Sometimes, a blackhead pops right out. Other times a pimple may burst. This might feel like it is getting rid of the blemish. However, squeezing pimples actually makes them worse. It irritates the skin and spreads the bacteria. This is the same bacteria that helped cause the acne in the first place. Squeezing a big zit on your forehead is setting yourself up for more pimples. Squeezing pimples can cause scars that are permanent and much harder to hide than pimples.

Okay, so squeezing zits won't make acne better. Then what will? There are some ways to keep acne under control. Most are things you need to do every day. Improvement may not be noticeable right away. Therefore, you should give a particular method several weeks to work. Acne starts under the skin's surface, so it may take a while for it to clear up completely. A person's face may even look worse before it gets better.

Help Yourself

Most of the things people can do to keep their skin clear of acne are easy. It is just a matter of getting into the habit of taking these steps every day.

Keep skin clean. Gently wash your face one or two times a day. Dirt, sweat, old makeup, and oil are acne agitators. Try to keep your hands away from your face. Hands usually are oily and dirty. Wash your face after exercise to get rid of sweat. Also, wash your face after work if your part-time job involves being near oil. Such jobs may include working at a fast-food restaurant or gas station.

Get out the grease. If your hair is limp and greasy, shampoo it every day. Oil glands in the scalp can work overtime, too. Oily hair on the forehead can cause zits. Try wearing your hair off of your forehead. Dirt and sweat can collect between the skin and a baseball cap. Not wearing a baseball cap may help hair look better and skin feel less oily.

Listen to your body. Acne is not directly caused by foods you eat. However, acne might seem worse after eating or drinking certain items. It can't hurt to avoid these trigger foods. Some people are more sensitive to foods than others are. One reaction could be a skin breakout.

Don't clog pores. If you use makeup or moisturizers, look for brands that are oil-free, noncomedogenic, or nonacnegenic. These words mean that the makeup or lotion should not clog pores. Also, shield your face with your hand when using hairspray or hair gel. Use a sunscreen that is oil-free, too.

A Few Words About Acne and the Sun

Many people think that acne improves after being exposed to sunlight. Some adults may even tell you that the sun dries your skin and pimples. This is a nice theory, but it is not quite correct. A tan may make a person look healthier. However, it also can make the skin around a blemish look darker. The sun's rays do dry the skin, but the body reacts by producing more oil from the sebaceous glands. This may cause more pimples later. Sun exposure also can lead to sun damage. This is discussed more in Chapter 6.

What Next?

Following simple, self-help steps should make acne better.
Blemishes might still appear now and then. You can hide
occasional acne with a little tinted acne lotion. Face powder mixed
with oil-free foundation works, too. You may even decide not to
worry about a zit because almost everyone else has a few, too.

Some people, however, still get many blemishes even after
following the self-help steps. These people should continue with
these steps. They also should see a doctor about acne treatment
that might help them. The doctor may start someone with lotions
and creams that can be bought over-the-counter, or without a
prescription. If these products don't work after two or three
months, the doctor may suggest prescription medicine. This is
medicine that only the doctor can give a person.

Skin Care

Every year, about 7 million Americans visit a doctor for advice on a new skin problem.

The important thing to remember is that you do not have to live with acne. First, work on your own. Then, work with your doctor. Also work on unhappy feelings that may creep up on you when you look in the mirror. Acne can make a person feel ashamed, discouraged, and embarrassed. Working to control acne can help a person not only to look better but also to feel better.

Points to Consider

Think about how you wash your face now. Would you change anything about the way you do it?

How do you think the sun affects acne?

What are some things you already do to control acne?

Most acne can be treated with over-the-counter medicines you can buy yourself.

Acne treatments clean, dry, and peel the skin. They unclog pores and kill bacteria. Nonprescription acne treatment ingredients include benzoyl peroxide, salicylic acid, or sulfur and resorcinol.

Some people feel that herbal remedies help lessen their acne, although no medical evidence supports this.

Chapter **4**

More Help for Acne

Scott walked down the aisle in the store. He thought there must

be a million different zit creams. He didn't know which one to try. His friend Yasahiro used one kind, but Scott's girlfriend, Amy, liked another one. He stared at the shelves and finally bought the one that was the least expensive.

Even people who are similar in age, gender, or race may not respond to acne treatments the same way. Everyone is different when it comes to acne.

Sometimes people need a little more help than do-it-yourself steps to control acne. Like Scott, you may think there are a million different treatments to try for acne. This is good because what works for one person may not work for another person. People may have to try several different creams, lotions, or cleansers before finding one they like.

Over-the-Counter Medicine

The first acne treatment to try is an over-the-counter, or nonprescription, medicine. Drug stores and other stores that sell skin-care products carry nonprescription medicine. Several different types of ingredients work on acne. These are peeling agents that dry the skin. Most ingredients work to reduce bacteria. Some of them may irritate skin.

People react differently to the ingredients in skin-care products. Therefore, a person should try one kind for six to eight weeks before moving on to another product. It takes approximately two months to make sure acne medicine has had a chance to work. However, if a rash develops, a person should stop using the product immediately.

The number of treatments available may make choosing one seem confusing. It is important not to rely on advertisements, cool packages, or even prices to make your decision. You can ask friends what they use, but remember, your skin may be different. Ask your doctor what he or she recommends. It is important to follow the medicine's directions carefully. Don't give up too early. Skin may even look worse than normal for a while as the medicine works. You probably have clogged pores that you can't even see. The medicine brings out the gunk in the pores.

What You Can Buy

Many skin cleansers say that they are for acne. Most do not do anything special as long as you are following the self-help steps in Chapter 3. Some cleansers may even make acne worse if a person is sensitive to that product. If you find a cleanser that works for you, go ahead and gently use it. The safest and most common cleanser is soap and water.

Experts recommend two common ingredients to look for in acne products. These are benzoyl peroxide and salicylic acid. Benzoyl peroxide kills bacteria that cause acne. Start with a gel, cream, or lotion that has a 2.5 to 5 percent benzoyl peroxide solution. This mild formula may be all you need. Use a 10 percent formula only if your acne seems too tough for the milder formulas. Benzoyl peroxide can really dry the skin. Benzoyl peroxide may take about two weeks to make any visible difference in the skin. It is not a cure. People have to use benzoyl peroxide until they outgrow acne.

Salicylic acid works in a different way. This acid tries to change the way skin cells shed. It helps unclog pores. Just like benzoyl peroxide, it needs to be used until people outgrow acne. If a person stops using salicylic acid, pores clog up again. Salicylic acid is a little less drying than benzoyl peroxide and can actually prevent blemishes before they happen. This ingredient can be found in lotions, creams, and pads.

Some products use a combination of two ingredients called sulfur and resorcinol. These products are less common than those that contain benzoyl peroxide and salicylic acid.

Natural Acne Control

No medical studies prove that any herbal remedies can help acne. However, some people still use these natural products to treat acne. They may try forsythia pod or honeysuckle flower to reduce swelling and redness. Some people use tea tree, lavender, or eucalyptus oils to try to kill skin bacteria. If you try an herbal remedy, it is important to use the right concentrations, or amounts; otherwise, they can irritate the skin.

Some herbal remedies can react with other medications a person may be taking. This could lead to unwanted and possibly harmful side effects. Before trying any herbal remedies a person should talk with his or her doctor.

Points to Consider

Have you or someone you know tried an acne treatment that contained benzoyl peroxide or salicylic acid? How did the medicine work?

Why do you think using mild soap and water is the safest, easiest way to clean the face?

How do you feel when your face breaks out? How do you think your friends feel when their face breaks out?

Chapter
Overview

It's a good idea to talk with a doctor before trying any acne treatments.

A doctor can help to create a treatment plan that includes effective products in proper amounts.

Doctors who specialize in skin disorders are called dermatologists.

In some cases, acne is treated with strong, prescription medications.

People should not pick at blemishes because scarring can occur.

Chapter 5

Doctors and Prescription Medicine for Acne

Ronn noticed some pimples on his forehead and chin. He went to **RONN, AGE 17** the drug store and bought a 5 percent benzoyl peroxide cream. He tried it for almost three months. It didn't seem to help much. Ronn decided to try a stronger cream. The pharmacist suggested a 10 percent benzoyl peroxide cream. After another three months, Ronn was frustrated. Not only was his acne still there, it seemed to be a little worse. Ronn's mother suggested he visit Dr. Oakley. The doctor gave Ronn a few other products to use together. She told Ronn, "We'll get you over this. It's just going to take a little more time and patience."

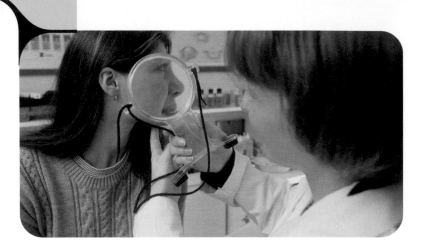

When to See A Doctor or Dermatologist

It's a good idea to talk with a doctor before using any acne treatment, even an over-the-counter one. A doctor can rule out other skin problems. Occasionally, makeup or medicine can cause a rash that may look like acne. In rare cases, serious hormone imbalances can cause acne. It also is important to see a doctor if:

Acne keeps you from doing things with your friends.

Acne causes scarring.

Pimples are large and painful.

Acne causes dark spots.

A doctor can help adjust the dosage of acne creams and create a treatment plan specifically for you. A typical plan might be to use the self-help steps in Chapter 3, along with some over-the-counter treatments. You might start with a cleanser that has salicylic acid and use a mild benzoyl peroxide lotion to smooth onto the skin. For some people, one product may be enough to control acne.

Try to keep a record of which products you use and how well they work. Just write down in a notebook what you try and how long you use it. Add a few notes about how your skin feels and looks after using a product, too. These notes may help your doctor if over-the-counter treatments don't seem to work. They may help the doctor decide which prescription medicine may work best for you.

Some people may not see any improvement after two months of self-help and over-the-counter treatment. At this point, the doctor may send the person to a dermatologist. A dermatologist is a doctor who is an expert on skin disorders.

Prescription Medicines

Dermatologists and other doctors can choose from several prescription medicines used to treat acne. Just like over-the-counter treatments, these medications may take a while to work. Some people may need to try several before finding one that works for them.

Creams, lotions, and ointments. A doctor might start with a topical treatment such as an antibiotic lotion, cream, or ointment. These antibiotics are rubbed directly onto the skin. They reduce inflamed, or red and swollen, pimples and kill skin bacteria. Retinoic acids are another type of topical treatment. Retinoic acids are vitamin A acids that help unclog pores and reduce bacteria. A doctor may prescribe antibiotics and vitamin A acids alone or together.

Oral antibiotics. Doctors rarely prescribe an antibiotic pill for acne treatment first. They usually suggest a topical treatment before an oral medication. An oral antibiotic is considered systemic. That means it travels throughout the body's system. An antibiotic helps reduce acne swelling and redness. Several such antibiotics commonly are used for acne treatment.

Birth control pills. Some women and girls who use birth control pills report that their acne gets better. The pills regulate hormone levels, so they could improve acne in some women. The Food and Drug Administration (FDA) approves one brand of birth control pill specifically for acne treatment. Experts say most brands should have the same effect on acne. However, other companies who make birth control pills have not completed research to prove this. That is why these other pills do not have official approval for acne treatment.

Tips about following a doctor's instructions:

Some people double or triple a doctor's prescribed dose of an oral medication. These people may think if one dose works well, more will work even better. However, taking extra medication is dangerous. The body may not be able to handle that amount of the drug. Side effects increase as well.

Some people think missing one or two doses of a medication does not matter. However, timing is important. It maintains the level of medicine that the body needs for it to be effective.

Some people use a topical medication more often than prescribed. This can irritate acne and increase inflammation.

Isotretinoin. This strong medication is used only as a last resort. Doctors prescribe isotretinoin only if all other treatments have not worked and if acne is severe. Isotretinoin commonly is known as Accutane®. Ninety percent of patients treated with isotretinoin are cleared of acne after five months. However, isotretinoin can cause severe side effects. The face may become very red. Skin may peel and crack. The drug can cause serious birth defects, so females must use birth control pills before, during, and after treatment. If sexually active, a female also must use a second type of birth control while taking this drug. Isotretinoin can cause dry skin, chapped lips, nosebleeds, blurred vision, headaches, and liver problems, too.

Corticosteroids. This type of medicine is used only in cases of severely inflamed acne lumps. It is injected into the lump by a dermatologist.

"I've had really severe acne for the last couple of years. My dermatologist just prescribed Accutane® for me. He told me not to take vitamin A supplements or multivitamins with high amounts of vitamin A. If I did, it could cause an overdose of vitamin A in my skin, bones, or liver."—Clay, age 16

Acne and Beyond

A dermatologist also should be seen if a person has a really bothersome pimple, cyst, or blackhead. It is important not to pick at these blemishes yourself. Picking at blemishes may cause inflammation and make acne worse. It also can cause scarring. Removal of acne blemishes is considered surgery. A dermatologist is familiar with surgical methods that can reduce acne scarring.

The American Academy of Dermatology (AAD) operates a toll-free number for information on acne and its treatment. It also can provide a list of dermatologists in your area. The number is 1-888-462-3376. Calls are answered 24 hours a day. For more information about the AAD and other organizations, see the Useful Addresses and Internet Sites section at the back of this book.

Points to Consider

How do you think severe acne would affect a person's life?

What are three different reasons a person should see a doctor for acne treatment?

Why do you think doctors usually prescribe topical treatments before oral medications for acne?

Many people today think a tan looks attractive and healthy.

Skin cancer is now the most common cancer.

There are three main things people can do every day to protect their skin: wear a sunscreen, cover up, and avoid the sun from 10:00 A.M. to 4:00 P.M.

A sunless-tan product can give the look of a tan.

Chapter 6

Sun—A Not-So-Healthy Glow

David is outside every chance he gets. He plays basketball on the courts at the park all summer long. He and his friends play volleyball at the beach every weekend. David works as a camp counselor to save money for college. In the winter, he skis and runs. David's skin is usually a golden brown.

DAVID, AGE 15

Today, a tan is considered attractive and healthy. You may hear people comment on how great someone looks with a tan. Some people may urge others to go outside and "get a little color in their cheeks." Before the early 1900s, having a tan was not fashionable. Skin cancer rates were much lower then, too. Skin cancer is now the most common cancer in the United States.

You probably have heard about the gloom and doom of the sun and skin cancer. It is a good idea to protect your skin from the sunlight that can cause skin cancer. However, you also should be concerned about the other invisible things sun can do to the skin. You may notice that some adults have brown spots, wrinkles, and sagging, leathery skin. Experts say that sun exposure causes almost 90 percent of these conditions. Skin does not look this way just because of age. Growing old does not have to mean getting wrinkled.

DID YOU KNOW?

It may be hard to think about what you will look like 10 or 30 years from now. People have to live longer with their skin as an adult than they do as a teen, though. Developing safe sun habits now can help your skin stay its healthiest and most attractive.

The Sun

When people are outside, the sun hits them with ultraviolet radiation. Two types of radiation break through the atmosphere to reach the skin—UVA and UVB rays. UVA rays go deep into the dermis and cause tanning. UVB rays burn the skin's surface. Most people can tell that a red, sore, blistering burn has damaged their skin. However, a tan is skin damage, too.

Rays from the sun speed up the body's cells that make melanin. The body responds to the sun by making more melanin to protect itself from the radiation. People have different amounts of melanin in their skin. Doctors use skin types to describe the differences. For example, Type 1 people are fair-haired, fair-skinned, and sunburn easily. People who are Type 5 or 6 have slightly more natural protection against the sun than other people do. However, they still need to protect their skin from the adverse, or negative, effects of the sun. See the chart on the next page for a list of all the skin types.

The color of skin and hair comes from a chemical in the skin called melanin. The more melanin a person has, the darker his or her skin. The cells in the skin that make melanin are called melanocytes. Interestingly, everyone, regardless of skin color, has approximately the same number of melanocytes.

The Six Skin Types

Type	Characteristics
1	Burns easily, doesn't tan, skin is extremely sensitive to the sun. Person often has red hair and blue eyes.
2	Burns easily, tans slightly, skin is quite sensitive to the sun. Often has blond hair and light-colored eyes.
3	Burns sometimes, tans gradually to a light brown, skin is somewhat sensitive to the sun.
4	Burns a little, tans to a medium brown, skin is slightly sensitive to the sun.
5	Burns rarely, tans well, skin is not as sensitive to the sun as types 1–4. Person tans to brown.
6	Does not burn, skin is not as sensitive to the sun as types 1–5. Person tans to dark brown.

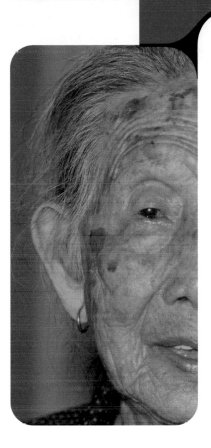

Other Ways the Skin Pays

Teens do not see wrinkles, age spots, blotchy spots, and sagging skin on themselves now. Exposure to the sun causes these conditions to appear sooner than usual. Sun exposure also can damage the immune system. This makes it harder for a person to stay healthy.

Protection, the Best Medicine

You can take three main steps to protect your skin from sun damage. These steps are not just for lazy days on the beach. Most dermatologists believe that about 80 percent of people's sun exposure occurs during everyday activities before age 18. It is important to work all the time to protect skin from the sun. Many acne medications make skin sensitive to the sun. Therefore, it is a good idea to talk with your doctor about what you should do.

Wear a Sunscreen

It is important to wear sunscreen all the time. This is true even if you are not planning to be outside for long. The best sunscreen has a sun protection factor (SPF) of 15 or greater and contains a UVA block. A sunscreen's SPF increases the amount of time people can stay in the sun without damaging their skin. The label should state if it is a broad-spectrum sunscreen. This type of sunscreen is best. A broad-spectrum sunscreen blocks both UVA and UVB rays. It also is important to look for a product that is hypoallergenic and noncomedogenic. That way you shouldn't break out or get a rash when you use it.

Sunscreen should be applied 20 minutes before sun exposure to set up properly in the skin. Then it should be reapplied every two hours. If you are in the direct sun, use a sunscreen with a high SPF number. For example, a high SPF helps when someone is lounging in a chair by a pool. Sunscreen should be reapplied after swimming or sweating. It is a good idea to use a waterproof and sweatproof sunscreen if you play sports. If you can't bring yourself to wear sunscreen every day, at least try to apply a moisturizer with sunscreen in it.

Skin Care

"It is so hard not to lie on the beach for hours in the summer with my friends. I used to want the best tan by the end of summer. Then my mom's friend showed me some pictures of my mom when she was in high school. I had no idea my mom's skin was so nice. She has so many wrinkles now, it's really sad. My mom looks like she could be my grandmother. I still hang out at the beach with my friends, but I wear sunscreen all the time. Whenever I am tempted to tan fast, I just close my eyes and imagine myself with my mom's wrinkles. No way!"—Chan, age 17

Cover Up

Covering up is another way to fight sun damage. One idea is to wear long-sleeved shirts and long pants or skirts. Wearing a wide-brimmed hat can help, too. Wearing sunglasses also provides protection. The type that provide almost 100 percent protection against ultraviolet rays are best. A little sticker on the glasses should state how much radiation they block. Some companies make special clothing specifically designed to block the sun. A dermatologist can make recommendations regarding these companies.

Avoid High Noon

The sun's rays are the strongest between 10:00 A.M. and 4:00 P.M. Planning activities so you are not outside much during these hours can help protect skin.

The American Academy of Dermatology conducted a survey. Of all the people asked, one-third said they never sunbathe and always use sunscreen.

The Only Safe Tan

You may not like the thought of wearing lots of sunscreen and covering up from head to toe. Perhaps you are afraid that you will look like a pale ghost compared with bronzed friends. You could try a temporary self-tanner if you want that summertime look. Self-tanners sometimes are called sunless tanners or tans in a bottle. Most places that sell skin care products carry them. Most of these products are easy to use and last for a few days. These tanning products come in spray or lotion form. You may even try to convince your friends to share a bottle with you.

Try to avoid going to a tanning salon for some quick color. The radiation from tanning beds can cause skin cancer. The radiation may be up to five times stronger than natural sunlight.

Points to Consider

Do you ever go outside just to tan? How do you think this affects your skin?

What are some things you can do now to help your skin look its best later?

What can you say to friends who want you to catch some rays? What could you do so you could still hang out with your friends but protect your skin?

Chapter
Overview

Taking care of your skin is a lifelong commitment.

Skin is important to how you look and feel. How your skin looks reflects your health.

Several long-term habits can help make sure your skin is its healthiest.

It is important to make skin self-exams part of your routine.

Chapter 7

Healthy Skin for Life

Taking care of your skin is a lifelong commitment. Such a
promise means your skin should look and feel healthy as long as
you live. Many skin-care steps improve a person's general health
and appearance. Healthy skin usually means a healthy body.
Healthy skin also can help a person feel better about himself or
herself.

"You should figure out your skin type before buying makeup and moisturizers for your skin. I used this easy trick to see if I had oily or dry skin. You wash your face with soap and water. Then wait about an hour. Next, take a tissue and gently press it to your face. If you see greasy streaks on the tissue, you have oily skin. If there are no marks on the tissue, then you have normal skin. You have dry skin if there are little skin flakes on the tissue or your face. You can have oily, normal, and dry skin all on the same face. It's called combination skin."—Tina, age 17

Skin Care

Darice has smooth, soft skin. She hardly ever gets zits, so her

DARICE, AGE 17

friends tease her whenever she gets one. Her friend Dolores constantly asks Darice what she uses on her skin to look so good. Darice tells her she uses whatever is on sale. Darice guesses she was just born with great skin.

Darice may have inherited some good skin features from her parents. She has healthy skin for many other reasons, too. Darice practices healthy skin habits without even knowing it. These skin-healthy habits can really make a difference.

Regular Maintenance

Exercise. Exercise can make people feel great and improve circulation. Good circulation gives the skin a healthy, pink color. It also speeds healing.

Eat right. A balanced diet is one loaded with fruits, vegetables, proteins, and grains. A balanced diet gives skin the vitamins it needs to look and work its best. Drinking six to eight glasses of water each day helps keep skin from becoming too dry. Water also helps the oil glands work normally.

Get plenty of rest. Beauty sleep is no myth. The body rests and recovers during sleep. Most teens need at least eight hours of sleep each night.

Avoid smoking. Smoking ages the skin. It causes wrinkles and age spots.

Use the right makeup. Try to avoid using old makeup. Use the cosmetics right for your skin type. Clean the face gently and carefully when removing makeup. Moisturize dry skin. Use makeup with sunscreen to protect skin from the sun.

Do skin self-exams. Once a month, take 15 minutes to look at the skin all over your body. You may need a mirror to see some areas of your skin. Look for any differences or changes on your skin. For example, look for a new spot or mole. If you see any changes, talk with your doctor.

Special Treatment

A few special treatments may help your skin feel extra special.

Relaxation. Slow down and take time to relax. Clear your mind. Stress can aggravate acne. Learning to relax can reduce stress. Some examples of relaxing activities are breathing deeply and listening to soothing music.

Massage. Try gently rubbing the skin with noncomedogenic lotion. Touch can ease tension and aches. The lotion can help keep skin smooth.

Facial. Treat yourself to a facial or face mask once in a while. Some facials clean and tone the skin. Other facials soothe acne.

Smoking for just 10 minutes decreases the body's oxygen supply for nearly an hour. Smoking also can add wrinkles to the skin.

Points to Consider

Do you think it's more important to look good now or to look and be healthy your whole life?

What are some things you are doing now that may affect your skin? How do you think your skin will be affected?

Take 15 minutes to look at your skin the next time you are in the shower. What do you see that you never noticed before?

Glossary

acne (ACK-nee)—a skin condition that results from clogging up or blocking the skin's oil glands

blackhead (BLAK-hed)—the top of a plugged skin pore that turns dark when it is exposed to air

dermis (DUR-miss)—the middle layer of skin

epidermis (ep-uh-DUR-miss)—the top layer of skin

evaporate (i-VAP-uh-rate)—when a liquid changes to a gas or vapor

follicle (FAH-li-kuhl)—a little sac in the body that usually contains a hair root

gland (GLAND)—a group of cells that produces a substance the body needs to work well

noncomedogenic (NON-kuh-mee-doh-jen-ik)—not likely to clog pores

perspiration (pur-spur-AY-shuhn)—sweat

pore (POR)—a tiny hole on the skin's surface

sebaceous gland (si-BAY-shuss GLAND)—oil gland usually in the hair follicles of your skin

sebum (SEE-bum)—an oily substance that the sebaceous glands produce

subcutaneous tissue (suhb-kyoo-TAY-nee-uhss TISH-oo)—the deepest layer of skin

tissue (TISH-oo)—a group of similar cells that form a part of a person, animal, or plant

whitehead (WITE-hed)—a plugged skin pore that bulges

For More Information

Branzei, Sylvia. *Planet Dexter's Grossology.* Reading, MA: Addison Wesley, 1995.

Inlander, Charles B., and Janet Worsley Norwood. *Skin: Head-to-Toe Tips for Health and Beauty.* New York: Walker & Co., 1998.

Robins, M.D., Perry. *Play it Safe in the Sun.* New York: Skin Cancer Foundation, 1993.

Watson, Amanda. *Natural Beauty: A Step-by-Step Guide.* Boston: Element, 1999.

Useful Addresses and Internet Sites

American Academy of Dermatology
930 North Meacham Road
Schaumburg, IL 60173
1-888-462-3376
www.aad.org/aadpamphrework/acnepamp.
html

Canadian Dermatology Association
Suite 521, 774 Echo Drive
Ottawa, ON K1S 5N8
CANADA
1-800-267-3376

The Skin Cancer Foundation
PO Box 561
New York, NY 10156
1-800-SKIN-490 (800-754-6490)
www.skincancer.org/home.html

4Acne.com
www.4acne.com
Contains links to acne information and
treatment resources

AcneNet
www.derm-infonet.com/acnenet/
Provides information on acne including its
social impact; Also contains a glossary.

Health Canada—It's Your Health
www.hc-sc.gc.ca/english/archives/
iyhealth/acnee.htm
Discusses acne medications and their risks

KidsHealth.org
www.kidshealth.org/tccn/bodymind/index.html
#body
Offers online articles on tanning and acne in
the Body Basics section

Skinema: Dermatology in the cinema
www.skinema.com
Shows that even celebrities do not have
perfect skin

Index

Index continued

menstruation, 14, 20
moisturizers, 27, 56

nerves, 9
nodules, 12, 13, 18. *See also* acne
noncomedogenic, 27, 50, 58

oil, 15, 17, 20, 26, 27
oil glands, 9, 16, 18, 19, 26, 57. *See also* sebaceous glands
ointments, 40

perspiration. *See* sweat
pimples, 10, 13, 15, 25, 27, 40, 42. *See also* acne; zits
    causes of, 17–18
    squeezing, 25, 42
pores, 6, 13, 17, 19, 20, 27, 33, 34, 40

radiation, 47, 51, 53
rashes, 8, 32, 38, 50
recording of skin condition, 39
relaxation, 58
remedies, herbal, 35
resorcinol, 30, 34
rest, 57
retinoic acids, 40

salicylic acid, 34, 38
scars, 14, 18, 25, 38, 42
sebaceous glands, 9, 14, 16. *See also* oil glands
sebum, 16–17, 18, 19
self-esteem, 9, 29
senses, 7
skin, 4–5, 10
    cancer, 11, 46, 47, 53
    cells, 8, 17, 18, 20, 34
    cleansers, 33, 38
    dermis, 8–9
    discoloration of, 8, 27, 38, 41

epidermis, 8
layers, 8–9
maintenance, 57
protecting from sun, 49, 50–51
self-exams, 57
statistics, 29, 34, 52
types, 47, 48, 56
smoking, 57, 59
stress, 14, 20, 58
subcutaneous layer, 9
sulfur, 34
sun, 27, 44–51
    covering up for protection from, 51
    damage to skin, 11, 27
    rays, 47
sun protection factor (SPF), 50
sunscreen, 27, 50, 52, 57
sweat, 6, 20, 26
    glands, 6, 9

tan (suntan), 46, 47, 51, 52
    self-tanners, 52
    tanning beds, 53
tea tree oil, 35
treatments, 30–35, 36, 39. *See also* medications

ultraviolet (UV) rays, 47, 51
UVA block, 50

vitamin A, 40, 42
vitamin D, 7

water, 5, 57
white blood cells, 18
whiteheads, 13, 15, 17. *See also* acne
wrinkles, 46, 49, 51, 57, 59

zits, 13, 20, 23, 25, 26, 28. *See also* acne; pimples